THE EASY MEDITERRANEAN DIET COOKBOOK

50 Recipes for Everyday Cooking

to Achieve Health Goals

Rafka Harb

Table of Contents

Introduction

The general consensus has become that the Mediterranean diet is the healthiest and most preferred plan to help you lose weight and improve your overall health. When compared to many other diets that are making the rounds, people have found the Mediterranean diet very appealing its category of food to eat and the easy way it can be implemented into your daily life. There's no need to count calories or macronutrients which people find refreshing when it comes to living by the Mediterranean lifestyle and making it a part of their healthy diet. This diet focuses on a healthy variety of fresh fruits, vegetables, seafood, and fish. It forces us to break away from all the red meat we would commonly eat because of the dangerous health risks that come with it. By knowing exactly what you can and cannot eat, it makes it very easy to plan your meals without having to weigh food portions or count calories every meal.

The History of the Mediterranean Diet

The Mediterranean diet comes from the dietary traditions of the people of the Mediterranean island region such as the

Greeks and Romans. The people of these regions had a rich diet full of fruits, bread, wine, olive oil, nuts, and seafood. Despite the fatty elements in their diet, the people of this region tended to live longer and overall healthy lives with relatively less cardiovascular heart issues. This phenomenon was noticed by American scientist Ancel Keys in the 1950s.

Keys was an academic researcher at the University of Minnesota in the 1950s who researched healthy eating habits and how to reverse the decline in American cardiovascular health. He found in his research that poor people in the Mediterranean region of the world were healthier compared to the rich American population which had seen a recent rise in cardiovascular heart issues and obesity. Compared to wealthy New Yorkers, the lower class in the Mediterranean lived well into their 90s and tended to be physically active in their senior years. Keys and his team of scientists decided to travel the world and study the link between the region's diet and the health of the people who lived there. In 1957, he traveled and studied the lifestyles, nutrition, exercise, and diet of the United States, Italy, Holland, Greece, Japan, Finland, and Yugoslavia. Twenty years later, he published his findings in a landmark study called "The Seven Countries Study." It evaluated the diets and lifestyles of these regions and was one of the first studies to notice the link between cardiovascular disease and diet.

Keys' research found that the dietary choices of the people from the Mediterranean region allowed them to live a longer lifespan and one that kept them more physically active compared to other world populations. The people of Greece, in particular, ate a diet that consisted of healthy fats like seafood, nuts, olive oil, and fatty fish. Despite the amount of fat in these sources, their cardiovascular health stayed consistent without the risk factors for a heart attack or stroke. His study became a guideline for the United States to set its own nutritional standards, and he became known as the father of nutritional science.

With Keys' work leading the way, further research and clinical trials have been conducted on the Mediterranean diet which gives evidence for its health-improving properties. Not only will you lose weight, but you could lower your LDL "bad" cholesterol, lower your blood pressure, and decrease and stabilize blood sugar levels. With a decrease in these signs of cardiovascular heart disease, you can greatly reduce your risk of suffering from heart attack, stroke, or premature death.

It's important to point out that the Mediterranean diet cannot alone bring about these changes to someone's health. It will depend on a variety of other factors in their lifestyle such as genetics, physical exercise, smoking, obesity, drug use, etc. Part of the combination of the Mediterranean diet is incorporating physical exercise into your life. That's how it goes from the Mediterranean "diet" to a Mediterranean "lifestyle" that truly mimics the people of that region. The people of Greece tend to live an active lifestyle with some sort of daily physical activity they partake in. Whether that is walking, sailing, rowing, swimming, or hiking, coupling that physical exercise that with a healthy plant-based diet is what can bring about the beneficial health results. In our current environment, physical activity could mean a session at the gym or even just a walk around the block. It doesn't have to highly intensive, but the important part is incorporating some sort of physical activity in your day, so you can truly gain the benefits of following this diet.

Before we begin listing a rudimentary list of what you can and cannot eat, it's important to highlight that the Mediterranean region consists of many countries with their own unique dietary choices. With this diversity comes many varieties of recipes that you can incorporate into your dishes as long as you are still following the healthy tenets of the Mediterranean diet. This gives a basic outline of which foods you should include on your shopping list and then you can look for recipes from there! What does the basic Mediterranean diet look like?

- Your diet should consist heavily of whole grain bread, extra virgin olive oil, fresh fruits and vegetables, herbs and spices, nuts and seeds, fish and seafood.

- You should moderately eat: poultry, cheese, egg, yogurt.

- You should try to rarely eat: red meat and organ meat.

- You should avoid the following: processed snacks, refined oils (canola oil or vegetable oil), refined grains (white bread), sugary drinks (juice, soda), processed meats (hot dogs, sausages, bacon), trans fats .

- You should drink: water, wine.

The Science behind the Mediterranean Diet

Most of the benefits of this form of diet come from a large number of plant foods associated with the diet. By incorporating a large number of fresh fruits and fresh vegetables in your diet, you are getting a high number of antioxidants and free radicals which are helpful for your body's cellular system and metabolism. The high intake of vitamins, minerals, and fiber you're getting from these plant sources can lower your risk of diabetes, constipation and bowel issues, and heart disease.

Since we've mentioned the Mediterranean diet's intake of healthy fats, it's important to go over why these are healthier for the body. Most of the fat is monounsaturated such as the fat you get from olive oil. This fat, found in nuts, seeds, and oil, tends to be healthier for the body compared to the saturated fat that is found in meat and poultry. A high amount of saturated fat is what tends to wreak havoc on the body's cholesterol and blood pressure.

By staying low in red meat intake, the Mediterranean diet harnesses protein sources from fish and seafood which are healthier for the body.

They are high in omega 3 fatty acids. The research regarding omega 3 fatty acids is recent, covering the last 20 to 30 years, but it's shown to be an essential element for vision and brain health, as well as fetal health if a woman is pregnant.

Adults are advised to consume at least 250 to 500 milligrams of fatty acids a day. Since most of us don't eat fish every day, you can get in the form of a fish oil supplement. With the Mediterranean diet, that won't be as necessary.

The people of the Mediterranean had easy access to fishing and considered fresh fish and seafood a staple in their diet. Not only are there so many varieties, but it also is much healthier for you than having red meat many times a week which tends to raise your cholesterol and clog your arteries.

You can still have red meat on this diet, but you should try to consume it more rarely and be aware of your portion sizes. And if you do have red meat, you want to ensure that you are also having healthy vegetables or whole grains along with it.

Along with food, it's important to note that drinking alcohol in moderation is a big part of the Mediterranean diet. Recent studies in the last decade have shown that moderate consumption of red wine could considerably lessen the risk of heart related diseases, gallstones, and diabetes (Type 2).

It's believed that red wine contains a component called resveratrol which has health benefits in animals and humans. With this consumption, it's important to note that it is to be moderate, about a glass a day for women, and 2 for men. But with it can come health dangers for pregnant women or birth defects in babies.

Many declare alcohol consumption as optional in the diet because some people may be restricted due to health or religious reasons.

We can't speak about the science behind the Mediterranean diet without speaking in length about extra virgin olive oil.

With the abundance of olives in the Mediterranean region, olive oil is essential for all their cooking needs. That includes baking, seasoning, frying, and as a fat element in salad vinaigrettes. But when it comes to olive oil, the best oil will be labeled as "extra virgin" because it is the most unprocessed version of olive oil, so the purest that is available. There are many components in extra virgin olive oil that make it such a healthy substance.

It contains a high amount of vitamin E which has anti-inflammatory properties for the body. It also has a high amount of phenol substances which contains similar health properties. Oleic acid is another property that is healthy for the heart.

It's present in significant amounts in olive oil as compared to other oil types. When it comes to the properties of olive oil, it's taken very seriously by the culinary community.

There's an International Olive Council that tests the levels of phenol and acidity in different brands of olive oil to ensure they qualify for the label of "extra virgin".

The rule when it comes to olive oil is to go with the old saying "quality over quantity." Most nutritionists will say that consuming 4 to 5 tbsp of olive oil a day should be enough for all your cooking needs.

That includes salad dressings, pan frying, baking, or seasoning your food. Olive oil should be kept away from direct sunlight and heat to avoid degradation of the oil.

When we see all these qualities of the Mediterranean diet and how they play out for the body, it's easy to see how this diet can help you improve your health. By including exercise in your routine, you are also gaining the possibility of better health and strengthening your heart and losing more weight.

Along with the health benefits possible, the ease of the Mediterranean diet appeals to many people. No counting calories, no measuring food portions, or keeping track of your daily macronutrients.

With this flexibility and simply knowing the right foods to eat and avoid, the Mediterranean can be a very easy lifestyle to follow if you are hoping to improve your health.

Breakfast

Mediterranean Pita Breakfast

Preparation Time: 22 minutes

Cooking Time: 3 minutes

Servings: 2

Ingredients:

- 1/4 cup of sweet red pepper, chopped
- 1/4 cup of chopped onion
- 1 cup of egg substitute
- 1/8 teaspoon of salt

18

- 1/8 teaspoon of pepper
- 1 small chopped tomato
- 1/2 cup of fresh torn baby spinach
- 1-1/2 teaspoons of minced fresh basil
- 2 whole size pita breads
- 2 tablespoons of crumbled feta cheese

Directions:

Coat with a cooking spray a small size non-stick skillet. Stir in the onion and red pepper for 3 minutes over medium heat. Add your egg substitute and season with salt and pepper. Stir cook until it sets. Mix the torn spinach, chopped tomatoes, and mince basil. Scoop onto the pitas. Top vegetable mixture with your egg mixture. Sprinkle with crumbled feta cheese and serve immediately.

Nutrition

267 Calories

41g Carbohydrates

3g Fiber

20g Protein

Hummus Deviled Egg

Preparation Time: 10 minutes

Cooking Time: 0 minute

Servings: 6

Ingredients:

- 1/4 cup of finely diced cucumber
- 1/4 cup of finely diced tomato
- 2 teaspoons of fresh lemon juice
- 1/8 teaspoon salt
- 6 hard-cooked peeled eggs, sliced half lengthwise

- 1/3 cup of roasted garlic hummus or any hummus flavor
- Chopped fresh parsley (optional)

Directions:

Combine the tomato, lemon juice, cucumber and salt together and then gently mix. Remove the yolks from the halved eggs and store for later use. Scoop a heaping teaspoon of humus in each half egg. Top with parsley and half-teaspoon tomato-cucumber mixture. Serve immediately

Nutrition:

40 Calories

3g Carbohydrates

1g Fiber

4g Protein

Apple Cheese Scones

Preparation Time: 20 minutes

Cooking Time: 15 minutes

Servings: 10

Ingredients:

- 1 cup of all-purpose flour
- 1 cup whole wheat flour, white
- 3 tablespoons sugar
- 1 1/2 teaspoons of baking powder
- 1/2 teaspoon salt
- 1/2 teaspoon of ground cinnamon

- 1/4 teaspoon of baking soda
- 1 diced Granny Smith apple
- 1/2 cup shredded sharp Cheddar cheese, reduced-fat
- 1/3 cup applesauce, natural or unsweetened
- 1/4 cup milk, fat-free (skim)
- 3 tablespoons of melted butter
- 1 egg

Directions:

Preheat your oven to 425 degrees F. Prepare baking sheet by lining with parchment paper. Combine all dry ingredients in a bowl and mix. Stir in the cheese and apple. Set aside. Whisk all the wet ingredients together. Pour over the dry mixture until blended and turns like a sticky dough.

Knead the dough on a floured surface about 5 times. Pat and then stretch into an 8-inch circle. Slice into 10 diagonal cuts.

Place on the baking sheet and spray top with cooking spray. Bake for 15 minutes or until lightly golden. Serve.

Nutrition

169 Calories

26g Carbohydrates

2g Fiber

5g Protein

Bacon and Egg Wrap

Preparation Time: 15 minutes

Cooking Time: 15 minutes

Servings: 4

Ingredients:

- 1 cup egg substitute, cholesterol-free
- 1/4 cup Parmesan cheese, shredded

- 2 slices diced Canadian bacon
- 1/2 teaspoon red hot pepper sauce
- 1/4 teaspoon of black pepper
- 4x7-inch whole wheat tortillas
- 1 cup of baby spinach leaves

Directions:

Preheat your oven at 325 degrees F. Combine the first five ingredients to make the filling. Pour the mixture in a 9-inch glass dish sprayed with butter-flavored cooking spray.

Bake for 15 minutes or until egg sets. Remove from oven. Place the tortillas for a minute in the oven. Cut baked egg mixture into quarters. Arrange one quarter at the center of each tortillas and top with ¼-cup spinach. Fold tortilla from the bottom to the center and then both sides to the center to enclose. Serve immediately.

Nutrition

195 Calories

20g Carbohydrates

3g Fiber

15g Protein

Orange-Blueberry Muffin

Preparation Time: 10 minutes

Cooking Time: 20 - 25 minutes

Servings: 12

Ingredients:

- 1 3/4 cups of all-purpose flour
- 1/3 cup sugar
- 2 1/2 teaspoons of baking powder
- 1/2 teaspoon of baking soda
- 1/2 teaspoon salt
- 1/2 teaspoon of ground cinnamon
- 3/4 cup milk, fat-free (skim)

- 1/4 cup butter, (1/2 stick) melted and cooled
- 1 egg, large, lightly beaten
- 3 tablespoons thawed orange juice concentrate
- 1 teaspoon vanilla
- 3/4 cup fresh blueberries (or thawed frozen but it takes longer to bake)

Directions:

Preheat your oven to 400 degrees F. Follow steps 2 to 5 of Buckwheat Apple-Raisin Muffin Fill up the muffin cups ¾-full of the mixture and bake for 20 to 25 minutes. Let it cool 5 minutes and serve warm.

Nutrition

149 Calories

24g Carbohydrates

3g Fiber

Choco-Strawberry Crepe

Preparation Time: 5 minutes

Cooking Time: 10 minutes

Servings: 4

Ingredients:

- 1 cup of wheat all-purpose flour
- 2/3 cup of low-fat (1%) milk
- 2 egg whites
- 1 egg
- 3 tablespoons sugar
- 3 tablespoons of unsweetened cocoa powder
- 1 tablespoon of cooled melted butter
- 1/2 teaspoon salt

- 2 teaspoons of canola oil
- 3 tablespoons of strawberry fruit spread
- 3 1/2 cups of sliced thawed frozen or fresh strawberries
- 1/2 cup of fat-free thawed frozen whipped topping
- Fresh mint leaves (if desired)

Directions:

Whisk the first eight ingredients in a large size bowl until smooth and thoroughly blended.

Brush ¼-teaspoon oil on a small size non-stick skillet over medium heat. Pour ¼-cup of the batter onto the center and swirl to coat the pan with batter.

Cook for a minute or until crêpe turns dull and the edges dry. Flip on the other side and cook for another half a minute. Repeat process with remaining mixture and oil.

Scoop ¼-cup of thawed strawberries at the center of the crepe and toll up to cover filling. Top with 2 tablespoons whipped cream and garnish with mint before serving.

Nutrition:

334 Calories

58g Carbohydrates

5g Fiber

10g Protein

No Crust Asparagus-Ham Quiche

Preparation Time: 5 minutes

Cooking Time: 42 minutes

Servings: 6

Ingredients:

- 2 cups 1/2-inched sliced asparagus

- 1 red chopped bell pepper
- 1 cup milk, low-fat (1%)
- 2 tablespoons of wheat all-purpose flour
- 4 egg whites
- 1 egg, whole
- 1 cup cooked chopped deli ham
- 2 tablespoons fresh chopped tarragon or basil
- 1/2 teaspoon of salt (optional)
- 1/4 teaspoon of black pepper
- 1/2 cup Swiss cheese, finely shredded

Directions:

Preheat your oven to 350 degrees F. Microwave bell pepper and asparagus in a tablespoon of water on HIGH for 2 minutes. Drain. Whisk flour and milk, and then add egg and egg whites until well combined. Stir in the vegetables and the remaining ingredients except the cheese.

Pour in a 9-inch size pie dish and bake for 35 minutes. Sprinkle cheese over the quiche and bake another 5 minutes or until cheese melts. Let it cool for 5 minutes then cut into 6 wedges to serve.

Nutrition

138 Calories

8g Carbohydrates

1g Fiber

13g Protein

Barley Porridge

Preparation Time: 10 minutes

Cooking Time: 20 minutes

Servings: 4

Ingredients:

- 1 cup wheat berries
- 1 cup barley
- 2 cups almond milk, unsweetened + more for serving
- ½ cup blueberries
- ½ cup pomegranate seeds
- 2 cups water
- ½ cup hazelnuts, toasted & chopped
- ¼ cup honey, raw

Directions:

Get out a saucepan and put it over medium-high heat, and then add in your almond milk, water, barley and wheat berries. Bring it to a boil before reducing the heat to low, and allow it to simmer for twenty-five minutes. Stir frequently. Your grains should become tender.

Top each serving with blueberries, pomegranate seeds, hazelnuts, a tablespoon of honey and a splash of almond milk.

Nutrition:

150 calories

10g fats

29g protein

Gingerbread & Pumpkin Smoothie

Preparation Time: 15 minutes

Cooking Time: 50 minutes

Servings: 1

Ingredients:

- · 1 cup almond milk, unsweetened
- · 2 teaspoons chia seeds
- · 1 banana
- · ½ cup pumpkin puree, canned

- ¼ teaspoon ginger, ground
- ¼ teaspoon cinnamon, ground
- 1/8 teaspoon nutmeg, ground

Directions:

Start by getting out a bowl and mix your chai seeds and almond milk. Allow them to soak for at least an hour, but you can soak them overnight. Transfer them to a blender.

Add in your remaining ingredients, and then blend until smooth. Serve chilled.

Nutrition:

250 calories

13g fats

26g protein

Green Juice

Preparation Time: 5 minutes

Cooking Time: 0 minute

Servings: 1

Ingredients:

- 3 cups dark leafy greens
- 1 cucumber
- ¼ cup fresh Italian parsley leaves
- ¼ pineapple, cut into wedges
- ½ green apple
- ½ orange
- ½ lemon

- Pinch grated fresh ginger

Directions

Using a juicer, run the greens, cucumber, parsley, pineapple, apple, orange, lemon, and ginger through it, pour into a large cup, and serve.

Nutrition:

200 calories

14g fats

27g protein

Snacks , Sides and Appetizers

Mediterranean Chickpea Bowl

Preparation Time: 12 minutes

Cooking Time: 13 minutes

Servings: 2

Ingredients:

- ½ tbs. of cumin seeds
- 1 large julienned carrot
- A ¼ cup of tomatoes (chopped)
- 1 medium julienned zucchini
- A ¼ cup of lemon juice
- 2 sliced green chilies
- ¼ cup of olive oil
- A ½ cup of chopped parsley leaves
- 1 minced clove of garlic
- ¼ tbs. salt
- ¼ tbs. cayenne pepper powder
- A ¼ cup of radish (sliced)

- 3 tbs. walnuts (chopped)
- 1/3 feta cheese (crumbled)
- 1 big can of chickpeas
- Proportionate salad greens

Directions:

Another ingredient that you will see on the Mediterranean Diet list is chickpeas. The Mediterranean Chickpea Bowl is a popular snack that can be enjoyed at all times. You can use fresh or canned chickpeas as per preference.

For the salad, you will have to make a special dressing that will make the dish tasty. You need to roast the cumin seeds on a dry pan. Make sure the heat is at medium.

When the seeds begin releasing the aroma, put the seeds in a different mixing bowl.

In this bowl, add the olive oil, garlic, lemon juice, and tomatoes. Also, add the cayenne pepper and salt, and mix well to blend in all the ingredients.

Take a big bowl and add the chickpeas into it. Then put in the sliced and chopped veggies, and parsley leaves.

Adding walnut pieces will add an extra crunch to the Mediterranean chickpea salad.

Put in the seasoning you just prepared and then, mix all the ingredients well.

Nutrition:

30g Carbohydrate

12g Protein

38g Fat

492 Calories

Hummus Snack Bowl

Preparation Time: 5 minutes

Cooking Time: 5 minutes

Servings: 2

Ingredients:

- 8 tbs of hummus
- ½ cup fresh spinach (coarsely chopped)

- ½ cups of carrots (shredded)
- 1 big tomato (diced)
- ¼ tbs. salt
- ¼ tbs. chili powder
- ¼ tbs. pepper
- 6 sweet olives (3 green, 3 black, chopped)

Directions:

The Mediterranean Diet will not be complete without the use of hummus. They don't indulge in fast food, but opt for fresh salad bowls, which are full of nutrition and goodness.

You can either prepare the hummus at home or purchase a jar that does not contain added flavorings and preservatives.

Take a large bowl and put in 6 spoonfuls of hummus into it. In this, put in chopped olives, shredded carrots, spinach leaves, and diced tomatoes.

Coat these vegetables with hummus properly.

After mixing the vegetables and hummus paste for at least five minutes, add in the chili powder. Make sure that it is evenly spread into the whole salad.

Lastly, add pepper powder and salt in the hummus-veggies mixture. You can taste the mixture and check the balance of all the ingredients.

Some also drizzle on some extra virgin olive oil onto the salad. This step is optional and can be omitted.

The Hummus Snack Bowl is a complete snack on its own. If you desire to add some texture to it, some freshly baked flatbreads or bread will complement the salad.

Nutrition:

43g Carbohydrate

12g Protein

10g Fat

280 Calories

Savory Spinach Feta and Sweet Pepper Muffins

Preparation Time: 10 minutes

Cooking Time: 25 minutes

Servings: 10

Ingredients:

- 2 and ½ cups of flour
- 2 tbs. of baking powder
- A ¼ cup of sugar
- ¾ tbs. salt
- 1 tbs. paprika
- A ¾ cup of milk
- 2 fresh eggs
- ½ cup olive oil
- A ¾ cup of feta (crumbled)
- 1 and ¼ cups of sliced spinach
- 1/3 cup of Florina peppers

Directions:

If you are looking for a Mediterranean diet snack that will not only fill your belly but will create an explosion of tastes in your mouth, then this is the ultimate option.

As the muffins will be baked in the oven, you need to preheat it to a temperature of 190 degrees.

Take a deep and large container. In this, put in the sugar, baking powder, salt, and flour. Mix all these dry ingredients properly and make sure there are no lumps.

In a separate container, you need to pour in the milk, eggs and the olive oil. Stir these ingredients so that they form one smooth liquid.

Carefully pour in the liquids in the container that has the dry ingredients. Use your hand to mix everything well, so that a thick and smooth dough is formed.

Then it is time to put in the crumbled feta, pepper and sliced spinach into the dough. Then spend some time with it to ensure that the new ingredients have mixed evenly into the muffin dough.

You can get muffin trays at the market. In such a tray, scoop out portions of the dough and place it into the muffin tray depressions.

Put in this pan inside the oven for 25 minutes. After cooling, the muffins will be ready for consumption.

Nutrition:

15g Carbohydrate

10g Protein

20g Fat

240 Calories

Italian Oven Roasted Vegetables

Preparation Time: 5 minutes

Cooking Time: 30 minutes

Servings: 4

Ingredients:

- 2 sliced medium onions

- ½ tbs. salt
- 1 tbs. Italian seasoning
- 2 sliced yellow squash
- 1/8 tsp pepper powder
- 3 minced cloves of garlic
- 2 sweet and large green and red peppers
- 2 tbs. olive oil

Directions:

Salads form a big part of the Mediterranean diet. The secret to the health and well-being of these people is due to their high vegetable and fruit consumption. If you want to acquire the healthy inner glow, then sacking on these roasted Italian salads will come in handy.

Mixing is an art, and the taste of the salad will depend on how well you mix the ingredients.

Take all the cut, chopped, minced and diced vegetables and put them in a large salad mixing bowl.

After this, you will have to add required amounts of salt, Italian seasoning and pepper powder in the vegetables.

Toss these ingredients for some time to ensure that everything has mixed well.

Then pour in the olive oil into this mixture and again blend well.

Place the marinated vegetables in a roasting oven and put it inside the microwave oven.

The oven must be preheated at 425-degree temperature. The baking will take no longer than 25 minutes.

After pulling out the tray from the oven, you can sprinkle on some extra cheese. This is optional and can be omitted.

Nutrition:

16g Carbohydrate

3g Protein

4g Fat

100 Calories

Greek Spinach Yogurt Artichoke Dip

Preparation Time: 10 minutes

Cooking Time: 10 minutes

Servings: 2

Ingredients:

- 1 tbs. olive oil
- 9-ounces spinach (roughly chopped)
- ¼ cup Parmesan cheese (grated)
- 14 ounces Artichoke hearts (chopped)
- ½ tbsp. pepper powder
- ½ tbs. onion powder
- ½ tbs. garlic powder
- 8 ounces sliced chestnuts
- 2 cups of Greek yogurt (fat-free)

Directions:

Preheat the oven to 350°F.

Chop artichoke hearts into bite-sized pieces. Mix all ingredients together and season with a pinch of salt; pour into a small casserole or oven-safe dish (about 1-quart). Sprinkle the top with extra mozzarella cheese.

Bake for 20-22 minutes, or until heated through and the cheese on top is melted. Serve warm with pita or tortilla chips.

Nutrition:

20.9 g Carbohydrate

16.3 g Protein

2.9 g Fat

170 Calories

Crispy Falafel

Preparation Time: 20 minutes

Cooking Time: 8 minutes

Servings: 3

Ingredients:

- 1 cup, Chickpeas (drained and rinsed)
- ½ cup, Parsley chopped with stems removed

- 1/3 cup Cilantro , chopped with stems removed
- ¼ cup Dill , chopped with stems removed
- 4 Cloves garlic (minced)
- 1 tbsp, Sesame seeds (toasted)
- ½ tbsp Coriander
- ½ tbsp Black pepper
- ½ tbsp Cumin
- ½ tsp Baking powder
- ½ tsp Cayenne

Directions:

Thoroughly dry your chickpeas with a paper towel.

Place the parsley, cilantro, and dill in a food processor.

Mix chickpeas, garlic, coriander, black pepper, cumin, baking powder, and cayenne.

Transfer the mixture to an airtight container and chill for about an hour.

Take out from the refrigerator and mix the baking powder and sesame seeds.

Scoop the mixture into a pan with 3 inches of olive oil over medium heat to create patties. Keep in mind as you create the patties that you are aiming to make 12 with the mixture.

Let the falafel patties fry for 1-2 minutes on each side.

Once your falafel patties are nicely browned, transfer them to a plate lined with paper towels to finish crisping.

Dip, dunk, fill, and enjoy!

Nutrition:

328 Calories

10.8g Fat

24g Protein

Onion Fried Eggs

Preparation Time: 15 minutes

Cooking Time: 91 minutes

Servings: 4

Ingredients:

- 11 Eggs
- 1 cup White mushroom
- 4 oz Feta cheese (crumbled)
- 1/2 cup Sun-dried tomatoes (chopped)
- 2 large Onion (sliced)
- 2 Garlic clove (minced)
- 2.5 tbsp Olive oil

Directions:

Put a pan with the olive oil over medium-low heat.

Once hot, stir onions and mushrooms into the oil.

Allow the onion and mushroom mix to cook for about one hour. Stir them every 5-7 minutes to ensure they cook evenly.

After the onions have browned, add the sun-dried tomatoes and garlic, and let cook for 2 minutes.

Once the sun-dried tomatoes and garlic are fragrant, spread all the ingredients out into an even, thin layer across the pan.

Crack the eggs overtop the ingredients already in the pan.

Sprinkle your feta cheese and pepper over top of the eggs.

Cover the pan with its corresponding lid and let the eggs sit to cook for about 10-12 minutes. Gently shake the pan at 10 minutes to check on the consistency of the egg yolks. Continue to cook until they reach your desired level of doneness.

Remove pan from heat and divide the mixture between two plates.

Nutrition:

360 Calories

27g Fat

20g Protein

Black Bean Cake with Salsa

Preparation Time:15 minutes

Cooking Time: 18 minutes

Servings: 10

Ingredients:

- 1 Fl oz. Olive oil
- 16 oz Onion
- 2-4 cloves Garlic
- Jalapenos
- 2 tsp Ground cumin
- 32 oz. Black beans
- 1 tsp Oregano
- 450 ml Salsa cruda

Directions:

Heat the olive oil in a sauté pan over low heat.

Add the garlic and onions, cook until soft. Do not brown.

Add the ground cumin and jalapeño. Cook for a few more minutes.

Add the oregano and beans. Cook until they are heated through.

Place the mixture in a food processor and blend in a puree.

Season well.

Divide the mixture into 2 oz portions. Form into small, flat cakes.

Brown the cakes lightly on both sides in hot olive oil in a sauté pan.

Serve 2 cakes per portion with 1 ½ Fl oz salsa.

Nutrition:

260 Calories

12g Fat

9g Protein

Pickled Apple

Preparation Time: 10 minutes

Cooking Time: 20 minutes

Servings: 6

Ingredients:

- 1/2 cup Water
- (3 ½ oz) Maple syrup
- 1/2 cup Cider vinegar
- Sachet:
- 3-4 Peppercorns
- 1/4 tsp Mustard seed
- 1/4 tsp Coriander seed
- 1/4 tsp Salt
- 2 Granny smith apple
- 1 tbsp Italian parsley

Directions:

Combine the water, maple syrup, vinegar, sachet, and sat in a saucepan. Bring to a boil.

Pour the liquid and the sachet over the apples in a nonreactive container.

Let it be refrigerated for 3-4 hours or overnight.

Drain the apples before serving and toss with the parsley.

Nutrition:

50 Calories

0.1g Fat

0.3g Protein

Baked Clams Oreganata

Preparation Time: 30 minutes

Cooking Time: 13 minutes

Servings: 10

Ingredients:

- 30 Cherrystone clams
- 2 Fl oz Olive oil
- 1 oz Onions (chopped fine)

- 1 tsp Garlic (finely chopped)
- 1 Fl oz Lemon juice
- 10 oz Fresh breadcrumbs
- 1 tbsp Parsley ,chopped
- 3/4 tsp Oregano dried
- 1/8 tsp White pepper
- 1/3 cup Parmesan cheese
- Paprika (as needed)
- 10 Lemon wedges

Directions:

Open the clams. Catch the juice in a bowl.

Remove the clams from the shell. Place them in a strainer over the bowl of juice. Let them drain 15 minutes in the refrigerator. Save the 30 best half-shells.

Chop the clams into small pieces.

Heat the oil in a sauté pan. Add the onion and garlic. Sauté about 1 minute, but do not brown.

Use half of the clam juice, then reduce it over high heat by three-fourths.

Remove from the heat and add the crumbs, parsley, lemon juice, white pepper, and oregano. Mix gently to avoid making the crumbs pasty.

If necessary, adjust the seasonings.

Once the mixture has cooled. Mix in the chopped clams.

Place the mixture in the 30 clamshells. Sprinkle with parmesan cheese and (very lightly) with paprika.

Place on a sheet pan and refrigerate until needed.

For each order, bake 3 clams in a hot oven (450 F) until they are hot and the top brown.

Garnish with a lemon wedge.

Nutrition:

180 Calories

8g Fat

10g Protein

Lunch

Caprese Chicken Dinner

Preparation Time: 10 minutes

Cooking time : 20 minutes

Servings: 6

Ingredients

- ¼ cup maple syrup or honey
- ¼ cup chicken stock or water
- ¼ cup balsamic vinegar
- 1½ pounds boneless skinless chicken thighs, fat trimmed
- 8 slices mozzarella cheese
- 3 cups cherry tomatoes
- ½ cup basil leaves, torn

Directions

Open the top lid of your Instant Pot.

Add the stock, balsamic vinegar and maple syrup; stir to combine with a wooden spatula.

Add the chicken thighs and combine well.

Close the lid and make sure that the valve is sealed properly.

Press MANUAL and set timer to 10 minutes.

The Instant Pot will start building pressure; allow the mixture to cook for the set time.

When the timer reads zero, press QPR for quick pressure release.

Open the lid, remove the chicken thighs, and place them on a baking sheet. Top each thigh with a cheese slice.

Press SAUTÉ; cook the sauce mixture for 4–5 minutes. Add the tomatoes and simmer for 1–2 minutes. Mix in the basil.

Add the baking sheet to a broiler and heat until the cheese melts. Serve warm with the sauce drizzled on top.

Nutrition:

311 Calories

13 g Fat

15 g Carbs

31 g Protein

364 mg Sodium

Pork Loin with Peach Sauce

Preparation Time: 10 minutes

Cooking time 10 minutes

Servings: 4

Ingredients

- 1 (15-ounce) can peaches, diced (liquid reserved)
- ¼ cup beef stock
- 1 pound pork loin, cut into chunks
- 2 tablespoons white wine
- 2 tablespoons sweet chili sauce
- 2 tablespoons soy sauce
- 2 tablespoons honey
- ¼ cup water combined with 2 tablespoons cornstarch

Directions

Open the top lid of your Instant Pot.

Add the wine, soy sauce, beef stock, peach can liquid and chili sauce; stir to combine with a wooden spatula.

Add the pork and stir again.

Close the lid and make sure that the valve is sealed properly.

Press MANUAL and set timer to 5 minutes.

The Instant Pot will start building pressure; allow the mixture to cook for the set time.

When the timer reads zero, press NPR for natural pressure release. It will take 8–10 minutes to release the pressure.

Open the lid and mix in the cornstarch mixture.

Press SAUTÉ; cook for 4–5 minutes. Mix in the peach pieces.

Serve warm.

Nutrition:

Calories:277

Fat:4.5 g

Carbs:28 g

Protein:24 g

Mushroom Tomato Beef

Preparation Time: 10 minutes

Cooking time: 18 minutes

Servings: 4

Ingredients:

- 1 pound beef steaks
- 1 bay leaf
- 1 tablespoon dried thyme
- 6 ounces cherry tomatoes
- 1 pound button mushrooms, thinly chopped
- 2 tablespoons extra-virgin olive oil or avocado oil
- ½ teaspoon pepper
- 1 teaspoon salt

Directions:

Rub the steaks with salt, pepper and thyme.

Open the top lid of your Instant Pot.

Add the bay leaf, 3 cups of water, and the steaks; stir to combine with a wooden spatula.

Close the lid and make sure that the valve is sealed properly.

Press MANUAL and set timer to 13 minutes.

The Instant Pot will start building pressure; allow the mixture to cook for the set time.

When the timer reads zero, press QPR for quick pressure release.

Open the lid and take out the prepared recipe.

Add the olive oil to the pot and SAUTÉ the tomatoes and mushrooms for 4–5 minutes.

Add the steak and stir-cook to evenly brown. Serve warm.

Nutrition:

384 Calories

21 g Fat

11 g Carbs

23.5 g Protein

664 mg Sodium

Seafood and Veggie Pasta

Preparation Time: 10 minutes

Cooking Time: 20 minutes

Servings: 4

- **Ingredients:**
- ¼ tsp pepper
- ¼ tsp salt
- 1 lb raw shelled shrimp
- 1 lemon, cut into wedges
- 1 tbsp butter
- 1 tbsp olive oil
- 2 5-oz cans chopped clams, drained (reserve 2 tbsp clam juice)
- 2 tbsp dry white wine

- 4 cloves garlic, minced
- 4 cups zucchini, spiraled (use a veggie spiralizer)
- 4 tbsp Parmesan Cheese
- Chopped fresh parsley to garnish

Directions:

Ready the zucchini and spiralize with a veggie spiralizer. Arrange 1 cup of zucchini noodle per bowl. Total of 4 bowls.

On medium fire, place a large nonstick saucepan and heat oil and butter.

For a minute, sauté garlic. Add shrimp and cook for 3 minutes until opaque or cooked.

Add white wine, reserved clam juice and clams. Bring to a simmer and continue simmering for 2 minutes or until half of liquid has evaporated. Stir constantly.

Season with pepper and salt. And if needed add more to taste.

Remove from fire and evenly distribute seafood sauce to 4 bowls.

Top with a tablespoonful of Parmesan cheese per bowl, serve and enjoy.

Nutrition:

324.9 Calories

12g Carbohydrates

43.8g Protein

11.3g Fat

Creamy Alfredo Fettuccine

Preparation Time: 5 minutes

Cooking Time: 25 minutes

Servings: 4

Ingredients:

- Grated parmesan cheese
- ½ cup freshly grated parmesan cheese
- 1/8 tsp freshly ground black pepper
- ½ tsp salt

- 1 cup whipping cream
- 2 tbsp butter
- 8 oz dried fettuccine, cooked and drained

Directions:

On medium high fire, place a big fry pan and heat butter.

Add pepper, salt and cream and gently boil for three to five minutes.

Once thickened, turn off fire and quickly stir in ½ cup of parmesan cheese. Toss in pasta, mix well.

Top with another batch of parmesan cheese and serve.

Nutrition:

202 Calories

21.1g Carbohydrates

7.9g Protein

10.2g Fat

Walnut-Rosemary Crusted Salmon

Preparation Time: 10 minutes

Cooking Time: 20 minutes

Servings: 4

Ingredients:

- 1 lb. or 450 g. frozen skinless salmon fillet
- 2 tsps. Dijon mustard
- 1 clove garlic, minced
- ¼ tsp. lemon zest
- ½ tsp. honey
- ½ tsp. kosher salt
- 1 tsp. freshly chopped rosemary
- 3 tbsps. panko breadcrumbs
- ¼ tsp. crushed red pepper
- 3 tbsps. chopped walnuts
- 2 tsp. extra-virgin olive oil

Directions:

Preheat the oven to 420 F/215 C and use parchment paper to line a rimmed baking sheet.

In a bowl combine mustard, lemon zest, garlic, lemon juice, honey, rosemary, crushed red pepper, and salt

In another bowl mix walnut, panko, and 1 tsp oil

Place parchments paper on the baking sheet and put the salmon on it

Spread mustard mixture on the fish, and top with the panko mixture.

Spray the rest of olive oil lightly on the salmon.

Bake for about 10 -12 minutes or until the salmon is being separated by a fork

Serve hot

Nutrition:

222 Calories

12 g Fat

0.8 g Fiber

4 g Carbohydrates

24 g Protein

256 mg Sodium

Quick Tomato Spaghetti

Preparation Time: 10 minutes

Cooking Time: 20 minutes

Servings: 4

Ingredients:

- 8 oz. or 226.7g spaghetti
- 3 tbsps. olive oil
- 4 garlic cloves, sliced
- 1 jalapeno, sliced
- 2 c. cherry tomatoes
- Salt and pepper
- 1 tsp. balsamic vinegar
- ½ c. Parmesan, grated

Directions:

Heat a large pot of water on medium flame. Add a pinch of salt and bring to a boil then add the spaghetti.

Allow cooking for 8 minutes.

While the pasta cooks, heat the oil in a skillet and add the garlic and jalapeno. Cook for an extra 1 minute then stir in the tomatoes, pepper, and salt.

Cook for 5-7 minutes until the tomatoes' skins burst.

Add the vinegar and remove off heat.

Drain spaghetti well and mix it with the tomato sauce. Sprinkle with cheese and serve right away.

Nutrition:

298 Calories

13.5 g Fat

10.5 g Fiber

36 g Carbohydrates

9.7 g Protein

Crispy Italian Chicken

Preparation Time: 10 minutes

Cooking Time: 20 minutes

Servings: 4

Ingredients:

- 4 chicken legs
- 1 tsp. dried basil
- 1 tsp. dried oregano
- Salt and pepper
- 3 tbsps. olive oil
- 1 tbsp. balsamic vinegar

Directions:

Season the chicken with salt, pepper, basil, and oregano.

Using a skillet, add oil and heat. Add the chicken in the hot oil.

Let each side cook for 5 minutes until golden then cover the skillet with a lid.

Adjust your heat to medium and cook for 10 minutes on one side then flip the chicken repeatedly, cooking for another 10 minutes until crispy.

Serve the chicken and enjoy.

Nutrition:

262 Calories

13.9 g Fat

0 g Fiber

0.3 g Carbohydrates

32.6 g Protein

405 mg Sodium

Chili Oregano Baked Cheese

Preparation Time: 5 minutes

Cooking Time: 25 minutes

Servings: 4

Ingredients:

- 8 oz. or 226.7g feta cheese

- 4 oz. or 113g mozzarella, crumbled
- 1 sliced chili pepper
- 1 tsp. dried oregano
- 2 tbsps. olive oil

Directions:

Place the feta cheese in a small deep-dish baking pan.

Top with the mozzarella then season with pepper slices and oregano.

cover your pan with lid. Cook in the preheated oven at 350 F/176 C for 20 minutes.

Serve the cheese and enjoy it.

Nutrition:

292 Calories

24.2 g Fat

2 g Fiber

5.7 g Carbohydrates

16.2 g Protein

Turkey with Basil & Tomatoes

Preparation Time: 5 minutes

Cooking Time: 10 minutes

Servings:: 4

Ingredients:

- 4 turkey breast fillets
- 1 tablespoon olive oil
- 1/4 cup fresh basil, chopped
- 1 1/2 cups cherry tomatoes, sliced in half
- 1/4 cup olive tapenade

Directions:

Season the turkey fillets with salt.

Add the olive oil to the Instant Pot.

Set it to sauté.

Cook the turkey until brown on both sides.

Stir in the basil, tomatoes and olive tapenade.

Cook for 3 minutes, stirring frequently.

Nutrition:

188 Calories

5.1g Fat

2.8g Carbohydrate

33.2g Protein

Dinner

White Wine–Sautéed Mussels

Preparation Time: 10 minutes

Cooking Time: 10 minutes

Servings: 4

Ingredients:

- 3 pounds live mussels, cleaned
- 4 tablespoons (½ stick) salted butter
- 2 shallots, finely chopped
- 2 tablespoons garlic, minced
- 2 cups dry white wine

Directions:

Scrub the mussel shells to make sure they are clean; trim off any that have a beard (hanging string). Put the mussels in a large bowl of water, discarding any that are not tightly closed.

In a large pot over medium heat, cook the butter, shallots, and garlic for 2 minutes.

Add the wine to the pot, and cook for 1 minute.

Add the mussels to the pot, toss with the sauce, and cover with a lid. Let cook for 7 minutes. Discard any mussels that have not opened.

Serve in bowls with the wine broth.

Nutrition:

777 Calories

82g Protein

29g Carbohydrates

1g Sugars

27g Fat

Chicken Shawarma

Preparation Time: 15 minutes

Cooking Time: 15 minutes

Servings: 4

Ingredients:

- 2 pounds boneless and skinless chicken
- ½ cup lemon juice

- ½ cup extra-virgin olive oil
- 3 tablespoons minced garlic
- 1½ teaspoons salt
- ½ teaspoon freshly ground black pepper
- ½ teaspoon ground cardamom
- ½ teaspoon cinnamon
- Hummus and pita bread, for serving (optional)

Directions:

Cut the chicken into ¼-inch strips and put them into a large bowl.

In a separate bowl, whisk together the lemon juice, olive oil, garlic, salt, pepper, cardamom, and cinnamon.

Pour the dressing over the chicken and stir to coat all of the chicken.

Let the chicken sit for about 10 minutes.

Heat a large pan over medium-high heat and cook the chicken pieces for 12 minutes, using tongs to turn the chicken over every few minutes.

Serve with hummus and pita bread, if desired.

Nutrition:

477 Calories

47g Protein

5g Carbohydrates

1g Sugars

1g Fiber

32g Fat

Paprika-Spiced Fish

Preparation Time: 5 minutes

Cooking Time: 10 minutes

Servings: 4

Ingredients:

- 4 (5-ounce) sea bass fillets
- ½ teaspoon salt
- 1 tablespoon smoked paprika
- 3 tablespoons unsalted butter

- Lemon wedges

Directions:

Season the fish on both sides with the salt. Repeat with the paprika.

Preheat a skillet over high heat. Melt the butter.

Once the butter is melted, add the fish and cook for 4 minutes on each side.

Once the fish is done, move to a serving dish and squeeze lemon over the top.

Nutrition:

257 Calories

34 Protein

1g Total Carbohydrates

1g Fiber

13g Total Fat

Mediterranean Lamb Chops

Preparation Time: 10 minutes

Cooking Time: 10 minute

Servings: 4

Ingredients:

- 4 lamb shoulder chops, 8 ounce each
- 2 tablespoons Dijon mustard
- 2 tablespoons Balsamic vinegar
- 1 tablespoon garlic, chopped
- ½ cup olive oil
- 2 tablespoons shredded fresh basil

Directions:

Pat your lamb chop dry using kitchen towel and arrange them on a shallow glass baking dish.

Take a bowl and whisk in Dijon mustard, balsamic vinegar, garlic, pepper and mix well.

Whisk in the oil very slowly into the marinade until the mixture is smooth.

Stir in basil.

Pour the marinade over the lamb chops and stir to coat both sides well.

Cover the chops and allow them to marinate for 1-4 hours (chilled).

Take the chops out and leave them for 30 minutes to allow the temperature to reach normal level.

Pre-heat your grill to medium heat and add oil to the grate.

Grill the lamb chops for 5-10 minutes per side until both sides are browned.

Once the center of the chop reads 145 degree Fahrenheit, the chops are ready, serve and enjoy!

Nutrition:

521 Calories

45g Fat

3.5g Carbohydrates

22g Protein

Broiled Mushrooms Burgers and Goat Cheese

Preparation Time: 15 minutes

Cooking Time: 5 minutes

Servings: 4

Ingredients:

- 4 large Portobello mushroom caps
- 1 red onion, cut into ¼ inch thick slices
- 2 tablespoons extra virgin olive oil
- 2 tablespoons balsamic vinegar
- Pinch of salt
- ¼ cup goat cheese
- ¼ cup sun-dried tomatoes, chopped
- 4 ciabatta buns
- 1 cup kale, shredded

Directions:

Pre-heat your oven to broil.

Take a large bowl and add mushrooms caps, onion slices, olive oil, balsamic vinegar and salt.

Mix well.

Place mushroom caps (bottom side up) and onion slices on your baking sheet.

Take a small bowl and stir in goat cheese and sun dried tomatoes.

Toast the buns under the broiler for 30 seconds until golden.

Spread the goat cheese mix on top of each bun.

Place mushroom cap and onion slice on each bun bottom and cover with shredded kale.

Put everything together and serve.

Enjoy!

Nutrition:

327 Calories

11g Fat

49g Carbohydrates

11g Protein

Tuna and Potato Salad

Preparation Time: 10 minutes

Cooking Time: 0 minutes

Servings: 4

Ingredients :

- 1 pound baby potatoes, scrubbed, boiled
- 1 cup tuna chunks, drained
- 1 cup cherry tomatoes, halved
- 1 cup medium onion, thinly sliced
- 8 pitted black olives
- 2 medium hard-boiled eggs, sliced
- 1 head Romaine lettuce
- Honey lemon mustard dressing

- ¼ cup olive oil
- 2 tablespoons lemon juice
- 1 tablespoon Dijon mustard
- 1 teaspoon dill weed, chopped
- Salt as needed
- Pepper as needed

Directions:

Take a small glass bowl and mix in your olive oil, honey, lemon juice, Dijon mustard and dill.

Season the mix with pepper and salt.

Add in the tuna, baby potatoes, cherry tomatoes, red onion, green beans, black olives and toss. everything nicely.

Arrange your lettuce leaves on a beautiful serving dish to make the base of your salad.

Top them with your salad mixture and place the egg slices.

Drizzle it with the previously prepared Salad Dressing.

Serve hot.

Nutrition:

406 Calories

22g Fat

28g Carbohydrates

26g Protein

Baked Orzo with Eggplant, Swiss Chard, and Mozzarella

Preparation Time: 20 minutes

Cooking Time: 1 hour

Servings: 4

Ingredients:

- 2 tablespoons extra-virgin olive oil
- 1 large (1-pound) eggplant, diced small
- 2 carrots, peeled and diced small
- 2 celery stalks, diced small
- 1 onion, diced small
- ½ teaspoon kosher salt

- 3 garlic cloves, minced
- ¼ teaspoon freshly ground black pepper
- 1 cup whole-wheat orzo
- 1 teaspoon no-salt-added tomato paste
- 1½ cups no-salt-added vegetable stock
- 1 cup Swiss chard, stemmed and chopped small
- 2 tablespoons fresh oregano, chopped
- Zest of 1 lemon
- 4 ounces mozzarella cheese, diced small
- ¼ cup grated Parmesan cheese
- 2 tomatoes, sliced ½-inch-thick

Directions:

Preheat the oven to 400°F. Heat the olive oil in a large oven-safe sauté pan over medium heat. Add the eggplant, carrots, celery, onion, and salt and sauté about 10 minutes. Add the garlic and black pepper and sauté about 30 seconds. Add the orzo and tomato paste and sauté 1 minute. Add the vegetable stock and deglaze the pan, scraping up the brown bits. Add the Swiss chard, oregano, and lemon zest and stir until the chard wilts.

Remove from the heat and mix in the mozzarella cheese. Smooth the top of the orzo mixture flat. Sprinkle the Parmesan cheese over the top. Arrange the tomatoes in a single layer on top of the Parmesan cheese. Bake for 45 minutes.

Nutrition:

470 Calories

17g Total fat

7g Fiber

18g Protein

Barley Risotto with Tomatoes

Preparation Time: 20 minutes

Cooking Time: 45 minutes

Servings: 4

Ingredients:

- 2 tablespoons extra-virgin olive oil
- 2 celery stalks, diced
- ½ cup shallots, diced

- 4 garlic cloves, minced
- 3 cups no-salt-added vegetable stock
- 1 (14.5-ounce) can no-salt-added diced tomatoes
- 1 (14.5-ounce) can no-salt-added crushed tomatoes
- 1 cup pearl barley
- Zest of 1 lemon
- 1 teaspoon kosher salt
- ½ teaspoon smoked paprika
- ¼ teaspoon red pepper flakes
- ¼ teaspoon freshly ground black pepper
- 4 thyme sprigs
- 1 dried bay leaf
- 2 cups baby spinach
- ½ cup crumbled feta cheese
- 1 tablespoon fresh oregano, chopped
- 1 tablespoon fennel seeds, toasted (optional)

Directions:

Heat the olive oil in a large saucepan over medium heat. Add the celery and shallots and sauté, about 4 to 5 minutes. Add the garlic and sauté 30 seconds. Add the vegetable stock, diced tomatoes, crushed tomatoes, barley, lemon zest, salt, paprika, red pepper flakes, black pepper, thyme, and the bay leaf, and mix well. Bring to a boil, then lower to low, and simmer. Cook, stirring occasionally, for 40 minutes.

Remove the bay leaf and thyme sprigs. Stir in the spinach. In a small bowl, combine the feta, oregano, and fennel seeds. Serve the barley risotto in bowls topped with the feta mixture.

Nutrition:

375 Calories

12g Total fat

13g Fiber

11g Protein

Chickpeas and Kale with Spicy Pomodoro Sauce

Preparation Time: 10 minutes

Cooking Time: 35 minutes

Servings: 4

Ingredients:

- 2 tablespoons extra-virgin olive oil
- 4 garlic cloves, sliced
- 1 teaspoon red pepper flakes
- 1 (28-ounce) can no-salt-added crushed tomatoes
- 1 teaspoon kosher salt
- ½ teaspoon honey
- 1 bunch kale, stemmed and chopped
- 2 (15-ounce) cans low-sodium chickpeas, drained and rinsed
- ¼ cup fresh basil, chopped
- ¼ cup grated pecorino Romano cheese

Directions:

Heat the olive oil in a large skillet or sauté pan over medium heat. Add the garlic and red pepper flakes and sauté until the garlic is a light golden brown, about 2 minutes. Add the tomatoes, salt, and honey and mix well. Reduce the heat to low and simmer for 20 minutes.

Add the kale and mix in well. Cook about 5 minutes. Add the chickpeas and simmer about 5 minutes. Remove from heat and stir in the basil. Serve topped with pecorino cheese.

Nutrition:

420 Calories

13g Total fat

12g Fiber

20g Protein

Roasted Red Pepper Chicken with Lemony Garlic Hummus

Preparation Time: 10 minutes

Cooking Time: 10 minutes

Servings: 6

Ingredients:

- 1¼ pounds boneless, skinless chicken thighs, cut into 1-inch pieces

- ½ sweet or red onion, cut into 1-inch chunks (about 1 cup)

- 2 tablespoons extra-virgin olive oil

- ½ teaspoon dried thyme

- ¼ teaspoon freshly ground black pepper

- ¼ teaspoon kosher or sea salt

- 1 (12-ounce) jar roasted red peppers, drained and chopped

- Lemony Garlic Hummus, or a 10-ounce container prepared hummus

- ½ medium lemon

- 3 (6-inch) whole-wheat pita breads, cut into eighths

Directions:

Line a large, rimmed baking sheet with aluminum foil. Set aside. Set one oven rack about 4 inches below the broiler element. Preheat the broiler to high.

In a large bowl, mix together the chicken, onion, oil, thyme, pepper, and salt. Spread the mixture onto the prepared baking sheet.

Place the chicken under the broiler and broil for 5 minutes. Remove the pan, stir in the red peppers, and return to the broiler. Broil for another 5 minutes, or until the chicken and onion just start to char on the tips. Remove from the oven.

Spread the hummus onto a large serving platter, and spoon the chicken mixture on top. Squeeze the juice from half a lemon over the top, and serve with the pita pieces.

Nutrition:

324 Calories

11g Total fat

29g Total Carbohydrates

6g Fiber

29g Protein

Desserts

Orange Butterscotch Pudding

Preparation Time: 10 minutes

Cooking Time: 15 minutes

Servings: 4

Ingredients:

- 4 caramels
- 2 eggs, well-beaten
- 1/4 cup freshly squeezed orange juice
- 1/3 cup sugar
- 1 cup cake flour
- 1/2 teaspoon baking powder
- 1/4 cup milk
- 1 stick butter, melted
- 1/2 teaspoon vanilla essence

Sauce:

- 1/2 cup golden syrup

- 2 teaspoons corn flour
- 1 cup boiling water

Directions:

Melt the butter and milk in the microwave. Whisk in the eggs, vanilla, and sugar. After that, stir in the flour, baking powder, and orange juice.

Lastly, add the caramels and stir until everything is well combined and melted.

Divide between the four jars. Add 1 ½ cups of water and a metal trivet to the bottom of the Instant Pot. Lower the jars onto the trivet.

To make the sauce, whisk the boiling water, corn flour, and golden syrup until everything is well combined. Pour the sauce into each jar.

Secure the lid. Choose the "Steam" mode and cook for 15 minutes under High pressure. Once cooking is complete, use a natural pressure release; carefully remove the lid. Enjoy!

Nutrition:

565 Calories

25.9g Fat

79.6g Carbohydrates

6.4g Protein

51.5g Sugars

Ruby Pears Delight

Preparation Time: 10 minutes

Cooking Time: 10 minutes

Servings: 4

Ingredients:

- 4 Pears
- Grape juice-26 oz.
- Currant jelly-11 oz.
- 4 garlic cloves
- Juice and zest of 1 lemon
- 4 peppercorns
- 2 rosemary springs

- 1/2 vanilla bean

Directions:

Pour the jelly and grape juice in your instant pot and mix with lemon zest and juice

In the mix, dip each pear and wrap them in a clean tin foil and place them orderly in the steamer basket of your instant pot

Combine peppercorns, rosemary, garlic cloves and vanilla bean to the juice mixture,

Seal the lid and cook at High for 10 minutes.

Release the pressure quickly, and carefully open the lid; bring out the pears, remove wrappers and arrange them on plates. Serve when cold with toppings of cooking juice.

Nutrition:

145 Calories

5.6g Fat

6g Fiber

12g Carbs

12g Protein

Mixed Berry and Orange Compote

Preparation Time: 15 minutes

Cooking Time: 15 minutes

Servings: 4

Ingredients:

- 1/2-pound strawberries
- 1 tablespoon orange juice
- 1/4 teaspoon ground cloves
- 1/2 cup brown sugar
- 1 vanilla bean
- 1-pound blueberries
- 1/2-pound blackberries

Directions:

Place your berries in the inner pot. Add the sugar and let sit for 15 minutes. Add in the orange juice, ground cloves, and vanilla bean.

Secure the lid. Choose the "Manual" mode and cook for 2 minutes at High pressure. Once cooking is complete, use a natural pressure release for 10 minutes; carefully remove the lid.

As your compote cools, it will thicken. Bon appétit!

Nutrition:

224 Calories

0.8g Fat

56.3g Carbohydrates

2.1g Protein

46.5g Sugars

Streuselkuchen with Peaches

Preparation Time: 10 minutes

Cooking Time: 20 minutes

Servings: 6

Ingredients :

- · 1 cup rolled oats
- · 1 teaspoon vanilla extract

- 1/3 cup orange juice
- 4 tablespoons raisins
- 2 tablespoons honey
- 4 tablespoons butter
- 4 tablespoons all-purpose flour
- A pinch of grated nutmeg
- 1/2 teaspoon ground cardamom
- A pinch of salt
- 1 teaspoon ground cinnamon
- 6 peaches, pitted and chopped
- 1/3 cup brown sugar

Directions:

Place the peaches on the bottom of the inner pot. Sprinkle with the cardamom, cinnamon and vanilla. Top with the orange juice, honey, and raisins.

In a mixing bowl, whisk together the butter, oats, flour, brown sugar, nutmeg, and salt. Drop by a spoonful on top of the peaches.

Secure the lid. Choose the "Manual" mode and cook for 8 minutes at High pressure. Once cooking is complete, use a natural pressure release for 10 minutes; carefully remove the lid. Bon appétit!

Nutrition:

329 Calories

10g Fat

56g Carbohydrates

6.9g Protein

31g Sugars

Fig and Homey Buckwheat Pudding

Preparation Time: 10 minutes

Cooking Time: 10 minutes

Servings: 4

Ingredients :

- 1/2 teaspoon ground cinnamon
- 1/2 cup dried figs, chopped
- 1/3 cup honey

- · 1 teaspoon pure vanilla extract
- · 3 ½ cups milk
- · 1/2 teaspoon pure almond extract
- · 1 ½ cups buckwheat

Directions:

Add all of the above ingredients to your Instant Pot.

Secure the lid. Choose the "Multigrain" mode and cook for 10 minutes under High pressure. Once cooking is complete, use a natural pressure release; carefully remove the lid.

Serve topped with fresh fruits, nuts or whipped topping. Bon appétit!

Nutrition:

320 Calories

7.5g Fat

57.7g Carbohydrates

9.5g Protein

43.2g Sugars

Chocolate Mousse

Preparation Time: 10 minutes

Cooking Time: 6 minutes

Servings: 5

Ingredients:

- 4 egg yolks
- ½ tsp vanilla
- ½ cup unsweetened almond milk
- 1 cup whipping cream
- ¼ cup cocoa powder
- ¼ cup water
- ½ cup Swerve
- 1/8 tsp salt

Directions:

Add egg yolks to a large bowl and whisk until well beaten.

In a saucepan, add swerve, cocoa powder, and water and whisk until well combined.

Add almond milk and cream to the saucepan and whisk until well mix.

Once saucepan mixtures are heated up then turn off the heat.

Add vanilla and salt and stir well.

Add a tablespoon of chocolate mixture into the eggs and whisk until well combined.

Slowly pour remaining chocolate to the eggs and whisk until well combined.

Pour batter into the ramekins.

Pour 1 ½ cups of water into the instant pot then place a trivet in the pot.

Place ramekins on a trivet.

Seal pot with lid and select manual and set timer for 6 minutes.

Release pressure using quick release method than open the lid.

Carefully remove ramekins from the instant pot and let them cool completely.

Serve and enjoy.

Nutrition:

128 Calories

11.9g Fat

4g Carbohydrates

3.6g Protein

Carrot Spread

Preparation Time: 10 minutes

Cooking Time: 10 minutes

Servings: 4

Ingredients:

- ¼ cup veggie stock
- A pinch of salt and black pepper
- 1 teaspoon onion powder
- ½ teaspoon garlic powder
- ½ teaspoon oregano, dried
- 1 pound carrots, sliced

- ½ cup coconut cream

Directions:

In your instant pot, combine all the ingredients except the cream, put the lid on and cook on High for 10 minutes.

Release the pressure naturally for 10 minutes, transfer the carrots mix to food processor, add the cream, pulse well, divide into bowls and serve cold.

Nutrition:

124 Calories

1g Fat

2g Fiber

5g Carbohydrates

8g Protein

Decadent Croissant Bread Pudding

Preparation Time: 5 minutes

Cooking Time: 15 minutes

Servings: 6

Ingredients :

- 1/2 cup double cream
- 6 tablespoons honey
- 1/4 cup rum, divided
- 2 eggs, whisked
- 1 teaspoon cinnamon
- A pinch of salt
- A pinch of grated nutmeg
- 1 teaspoon vanilla essence
- 8 croissants, torn into pieces
- 1 cup pistachios, toasted and chopped

Directions

Spritz a baking pan with cooking spray and set it aside.

In a mixing bowl, whisk the eggs, double cream, honey, rum, cinnamon, salt, nutmeg, and vanilla; whisk until everything is well incorporated.

Place the croissants in the prepared baking dish. Pour the custard over your croissants. Fold in the pistachios and press with a wide spatula.

Add 1 cup of water and metal rack to the inner pot of your Instant Pot. Lower the baking dish onto the rack.

Secure the lid. Choose the "Manual" mode and cook for 12 minutes at High pressure. Once cooking is complete, use a quick pressure release; carefully remove the lid.

Serve at room temperature or cold. Bon appétit!

Nutrition:

513 Calories

27.9g Fat

50.3g Carbohydrates

12.5g Protein

25.7g Sugars

3.8g Fiber

Poached Apples with Greek Yogurt and Granola

Preparation Time: 5 minutes

Cooking Time: 15 minutes

Servings: 4

Ingredients :

- 4 medium-sized apples, peeled
- 1/2 cup brown sugar
- 1 vanilla bean
- 1 cinnamon stick
- 1/2 cup cranberry juice
- 1 cup water
- 1/2 cup 2% Greek yogurt
- 1/2 cup granola

Directions

Add the apples, brown sugar, water, cranberry juice, vanilla bean, and cinnamon stick to the inner pot of your Instant Pot.

Secure the lid. Choose the "Manual" mode and cook for 5 minutes at High pressure. Once cooking is complete, use a natural pressure release for 5 minutes; carefully remove the lid. Reserve poached apples.

Press the "Sauté" button and let the sauce simmer on "Less" mode until it has thickened.

Place the apples in serving bowls. Add the syrup and top each apple with granola and Greek yogurt. Enjoy!

Nutrition:

247 Calories

3.1g Fat

52.6g Carbohydrates

3.5g Protein

40g Sugars

5.3g Fiber

Jasmine Rice Pudding with Cranberries

Preparation Time: 5 minutes

Cooking Time: 15 minutes

Servings :4

Ingredients :

- 1 cup apple juice
- 1 heaping tablespoon honey
- 1/3 cup granulated sugar
- 1 ½ cups jasmine rice
- 1 cup water
- 1/4 teaspoon ground cinnamon
- 1/4 teaspoon ground cloves
- 1/3 teaspoon ground cardamom
- 1 teaspoon vanilla extract
- 3 eggs, well-beaten
- 1/2 cup cranberries

Directions:

Thoroughly combine the apple juice, honey, sugar, jasmine rice water, and spices in the inner pot of your Instant Pot.

Secure the lid. Choose the "Manual" mode and cook for 4 minutes at High pressure. Once cooking is complete, use a natural pressure release for 5 minutes; carefully remove the lid.

Press the "Sauté" button and fold in the eggs. Cook on "Less" mode until heated through.

Ladle into individual bowls and top with dried cranberries. Enjoy!

Nutrition:

402 Calories

3.6g Fat

81.1g Carbs

8.9g Protein

22.3g Sugars

2.2g Fiber

Conclusion

Thank you so much for reading! I hope that you have a greater understanding of the history and the science behind the Mediterranean diet, particularly with regards to all of the individuals who made significant contributions to uncovering more insights into the logistics of the diet.

However, more importantly, I hope that you are able to understand the importance of the research that went into discoveries of why someone who is trying to reduce their overall figure would want to seriously consider following the diet.

Each person's journey with regards to losing the amount of weight that they want is inherently unique, therefore, if you find that you are struggling in some way for whatever reason, do not give up hope.

The reality is that struggles are a part of life, and sometimes it can take a long time to curb some of the more negative habits that you have developed in the past.

Thus, if there is anything that you should take away from this is that the key to living a long and fulfilling life is to be conscious of yourself and the behavioral habits that you do so that you are able to work on improving any negative behaviors for the better.

Lightning Source UK Ltd.
Milton Keynes UK
UKHW020701310521
384670UK00006B/202